Objects in the Sky

The Daytime Sky 2
The Nighttime Sky 4
Day and Night 6
Changes in the Moon 8
Exploring the Moon 10

Harcourt

SCHOOL PUBLISHERS

Orlando   Austin   New York   San Diego   Toronto   London

Visit *The Learning Site!*
www.harcourtschool.com

The Daytime Sky

In the daytime sky you may see clouds. You may see the sun.

The sun is a star.
A star gives off its own light.

The Nighttime Sky

In the nighttime sky you may see stars. You may see planets and the moon.

The moon is a huge ball of rock.
It does not give off its own light.

Day and Night

The sun seems to move in the sky.
It does not move. Earth moves.

The Earth rotates, or spins like a top.
The part facing the sun has day.

Changes in the Moon

The moon's shape seems to change.
The changes make a pattern.

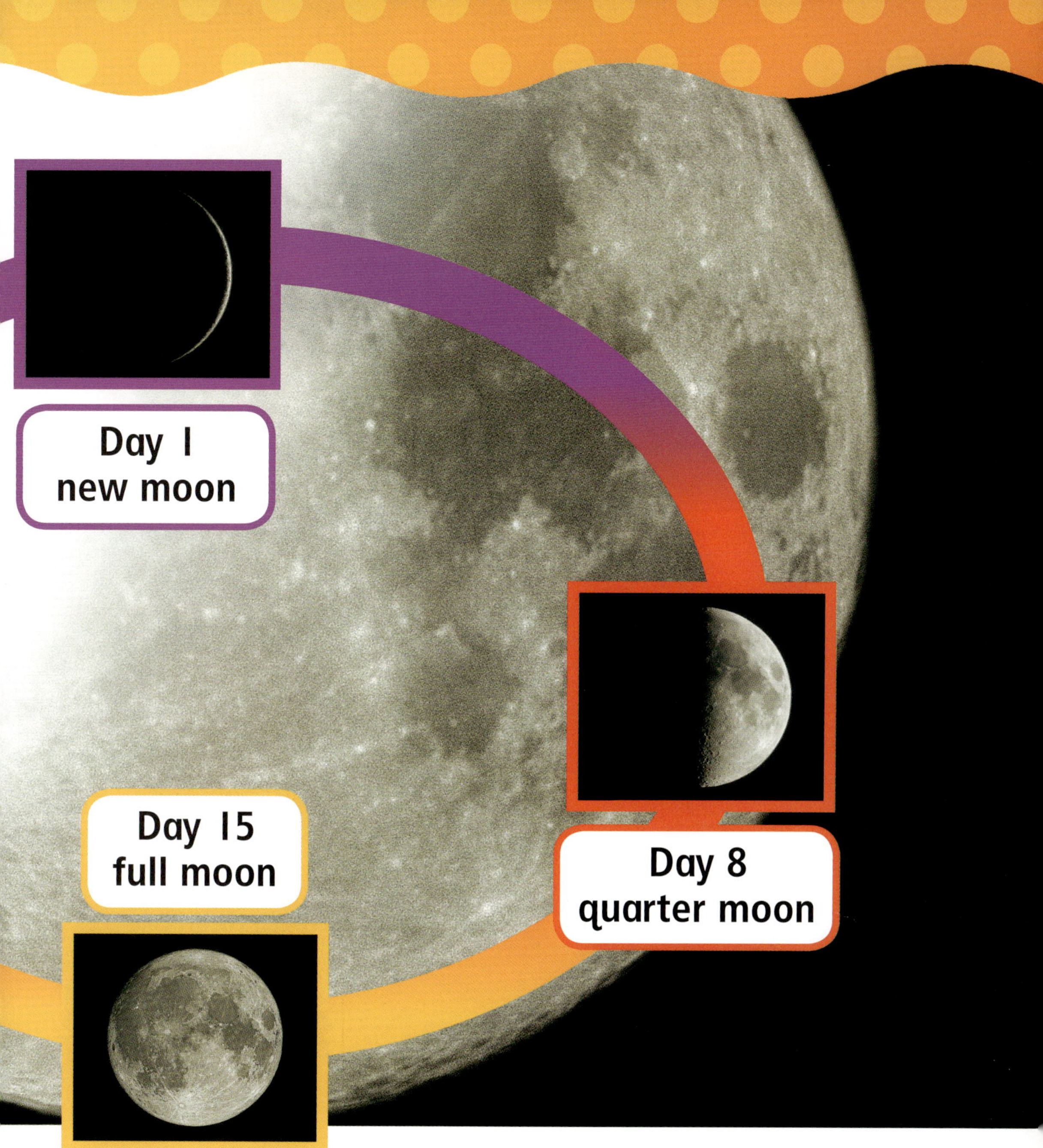

The pattern takes about 29 days.
After about 29 days, it repeats.

Exploring the Moon

Astronauts went to the moon in 1969 . They saw the moon's gray dust.

They saw craters and rocks.
Craters are holes shaped like bowls.

Vocabulary

sun, p. 2
star, p. 3
moon, p. 4
rotate, p. 7
crater, p. 11